LANGUAGE ARTS

Learning About

Nonfiction

by Martha E. H. Rustad

Consulting Editor: Gail Saunders-Smith, PhD

Consultant: Kelly Boswell, educational consultant

CAPSTONE PRESS
a capstone imprint

Pebble Plus is published by Capstone Press,
1710 Roe Crest Drive, North Mankato, Minnesota 56003
www.capstonepub.com

Library of Congress Cataloging-in-Publication Data
Rustad, Martha E. H. (Martha Elizabeth Hillman), 1975–
 Learning about nonfiction / Martha E. H. Rustad.
    pages cm.—(Language arts)
 Includes bibliographical references and index.
 ISBN 978-1-4914-0579-6 (hb)—ISBN 978-1-4914-0613-7 (eb)—ISBN 978-1-4914-0647-2 (pb)
1. Authorship—Juvenile literature. 2. Report writing—Juvenile literature. I. Title.
 PN159.R76 2015
 808.02—dc23   2014001861

Editorial Credits
Erika L. Shores, editor; Terri Poburka, designer; Charmaine Whitman, production specialist; Sarah Schuette, studio stylist; Marcy Morin, studio scheduler

Photo Credits
All photographs by Capstone Studio: Karon Dubke, except Shutterstock: paulaphoto, cover (girl), Rashevskyi Viacheslav, cover (shark)

The Little Explorer *Sharks* book is published by Capstone in partnership with Smithsonian.

For Lois.—MEHR

Note to Parents and Teachers

The Language Arts set supports Common Core State Standards for Language Arts related to craft and structure, to text types and writing purpose, and to research for building and presenting knowledge. This book describes and illustrates nonfiction. The images support early readers in understanding the text. The repetition of words and phrases helps early readers learn new words. This book also introduces early readers to subject-specific vocabulary words, which are defined in the Glossary section. Early readers may need assistance to read some words and to use the Table of Contents, Glossary, Read More, Internet Sites, Critical Thinking Using the Common Core, and Index sections of the book.

Printed in the United States of America in North Mankato, Minnesota.
032014   008087CGF14

Table of Contents

Look It Up

I wonder how fast a shark can swim. What does evaporate mean? Where is the Rio Grande? Look it up! A nonfiction book tells you facts.

At the Front

On the front cover, you will
find the author's name.
An author researches and
writes a nonfiction book.

Smithsonian
LITTLE EXPLORER
BIG FINS! SHARP TEETH!
Sharks may look scary, but they are simply fish! Find out all about these fascinating ocean creatures.
with Little Explorer
CORAL REEFS
BODY
SPACE
Water
Capstone Press
Smithsonian
Peterson
SHARKS
Capstone
Smithsonian LITTLE EXPLORER
SHARKS
by Megan Cooley Peterson

Turn to the table of contents.

It shows how topics are

grouped in the book.

Where do sharks live?

We can find out on page 6.

TABLE OF CONTENTS

In the Book

Headings tell readers what a section will be about. Find the heading "Speedy Swimmers." The words on these pages describe how sharks swim fast.

SPEEDY SWIMMERS

SWOOSH! Sharks move their heads from side to side when they swim.

Sharks can't swim backward.

FINS

DORSAL and **PELVIC FINS** keep the shark upright.

The **CAUDAL FIN** pushes the shark through the water.

PECTORAL FINS lift the shark through the water as it swims.

A shark's skeleton is made of cartilage instead of bone. Flexible cartilage makes swimming easier. Your nose and ears are also made of cartilage.

▲ The shortfin mako is the fastest shark. It darts through the water at 40 miles (64 kilometers) per hour or more.

10

Charts and diagrams help nonfiction readers.

Charts list facts in rows.

Diagrams use labels to show parts of something.

FROM PUP

Almost half of all ty

The rest give birth

egg

All shark pups
grow on their

18

SPEEDY SWIMMERS

SWOOSH! Sharks move their heads from side to side when they swim.

Sharks can't swim backward.

diagram

FINS

DORSAL and **PELVIC FINS** keep the shark upright.

The **CAUDAL FIN** pushes the shark through the water.

PECTORAL FINS lift the shark through the water as it swims.

A shark's skeleton is made of cartilage instead of bone. Flexible cartilage makes swimming easier. Your nose and ears are also made of cartilage.

▲ The shortfin mako is the fastest shark. It darts through the water at 40 miles (64 kilometers) per hour or more.

Many female sharks lay eggs in tough cases. These cases keep the young safe before they hatch.

...me types may live much longer.

chart

PUPS IN A LITTER	
bull sharks	7 to 12 pups
lemon sharks	6 to 18 pups
piked dogfish	2 to 16 pups

Maps tell nonfiction readers

where to find places. Look at

the United States map. The key

tells what map symbols mean.

I see a river. It's the Rio Grande.

The United States

Key
- ⌇ River
- ★ Capital
- • City
- ⌇ State

N W E S

At the Back

Nonfiction books have
more information at the back.

A glossary is a list of words
and what the words mean.

What does evaporate mean?

Glossary

condensation—the act of turning from a gas into a liquid

crop—a plant grown in large amounts; crops usually are grown for food

drought—a long period of weather with little or no rainfall

evaporate—the action of a liquid changing into a gas; heat causes water to evaporate

flood—to overflow with water

particle—a tiny piece of something; water droplets stick to dust, salt, and other tiny particles in the air to form clouds

water vapor—water in the form of a gas; water vapor is made of bits of water that cannot be seen

Read More

Goldsmith, Mike. *The Weather. Now We Know About.* New York: Crabtree Pub., 2010.

Higginson, Sheila Sweeny. *Drip, Drop! The Rain Won't Stop! Your Turn, My Turn Reader.* New York: Simon Spotlight, 2010.

Salas, Laura Purdie. *Colors of Weather. Colors All Around.* Mankato, Minn.: Capstone Press, 2011.

Internet Sites

FactHound offers a safe, fun way to find Internet sites related to this book. All of the sites on FactHound have been researched by our staff.

Here's all you do:

Visit www.facthound.com

Type in this code: 9781429660556

Super-cool stuff!

Check out projects, games and lots more at www.capstonekids.com

Bibliographies and indexes help readers too. A bibliography in a book about sharks lists other shark books. An index helps you find information within the book.

Index

Word Count: 180
Grade: 1
Early-Intervention Level: 18

Kinds of Nonfiction

Biographies and how-to books are kinds of nonfiction. Learn to make paper crafts from a how-to book. Read about the president in a biography.

Glossary

author—someone who writes books

bibliography—a list of books that tell more about a topic

biography—a book that tells about someone's life

chart—facts or information written in rows and lines

diagram—a picture that shows how something works

glossary—a list of words and what they mean

heading—a title at the beginning of a page or section

index—a list at the back of the book showing topics and their page numbers

key—a box showing what map symbols mean

map—a drawing of a place

table of contents—a list at the front of a book showing main ideas and their page numbers

Read More

Pelleschi, Andrea. *Neil and Nan Build Narrative Nonfiction.* Writing Builders. Chicago: Norwood House Press, 2014.

Rosinsky, Natalie M. *Write Your Own Nonfiction.* Write Your Own. Minneapolis: Compass Point Books, 2009.

Rustad, Martha E. H. *The Parts of a Book.* Wonderful World of Reading. North Mankato, Minn.: Capstone Press, 2013.

Internet Sites

FactHound offers a safe, fun way to find Internet sites related to this book. All of the sites on FactHound have been researched by our staff.

Here's all you do:

Visit *www.facthound.com*

Type in this code: 9781491405796

Check out projects, games and lots more at
www.capstonekids.com

Critical Thinking Using the Common Core

1. Why is the table of contents an important part of a nonfiction book? (Key Ideas and Details)

2. You want to know whether or not a certain fact is inside a nonfiction book. Describe two features of that nonfiction book that could help you find the fact. (Integration of Knowledge and Ideas)

Index

Word Count: 216
Grade: 1
Early-Intervention Level: 18